It's apparent the authr ... heart and soul into this book, both a personal and spiritual reflection on his life and how choice can make all the difference.
>   **Rev. Dr. Daniel Kanter,** Senior Minister
>   of First Unitarian Church of Dallas

Abramson has presented an approach that allows us to explore for ourselves some of the biggest questions that stand in the way of us having a life we want.
>   **Alice V. Ruffel,** PsyD., Clinical Psychologist

If you choose to read this book, you may discover what is holding you back in life, and what you can do to make your life more fulfilling.
>   **Steven Lane Taylor,** author of *Row, Row, Row Your Boat: A Guide to Living Life in the Divine Flow*

N.G. ABRAMSON

YOU CAN CHOOSE YOUR LIFE

A Guide to Experiencing More Peace, Freedom, and Happiness Right Now

You Can Choose Your Life
A Guide to Experiencing More Peace, Freedom, and Happiness Right Now

Copyright © 2019, N. G. Abramson

The views expressed by the author in reference to specific people in their book represent entirely their own individual opinions and are not in any way reflective of the views of Transformation Catalyst Books, LLC. We assume no responsibility for errors, omissions, or contradictory interpretation of the subject matter herein.

Transformation Catalyst Books, LLC does not warrant the performance, effectiveness, or applicability of any websites listed in or linked to this publication. The purchaser or reader of this publication assumes responsibility of the use of these materials and information. Transformation Catalyst Books, LLC shall in no event be held liable to any party for any direct, indirect, punitive, special, incidental, or any other consequential damages arising directly or indirectly from any use of this material. Techniques and processes given in this book are not to be used in place of medical or other professional advice.

No part of this book may be reproduced or transmitted in any form, or by any means, electronic or mechanical, including photography, recording, or in any information storage or retrieval system without written permission from the author or publisher, except in the case of brief quotations embodied in articles and reviews.

Published by:
Capucia, LLC
211 Pauline Drive #513
York, PA 17402
www.capuciapublishing.com

ISBN: 978-1-945252-41-9
Library of Congress Control Number: 2018957585

Cover design: Ranilo Cabo
Layout and typesetting: Ranilo Cabo
Editor: Simon Whaley
Proofreader: Simon Whaley
Book Midwife: Carrie Jareed

Printed in the United States of America

COPYRIGHT ACKNOWLEDGMENTS

Grateful acknowledgment is made to the following publishers for permission to quote from sources protected by copyright.

Oberlin Press for "The Judgment" from *The Intuitive Journey and Other Works* by Russell Edson. Copyright © 1976 by Russell Edson. Published by Harper & Row.

Houghton Mifflin Harcourt Publishing Company for an excerpt from "East Coker," in *Four Quartets* by T. S. Eliot. Copyright 1940 by T. S. Eliot. Copyright © renewed by Esme Valerie Eliot. Reprinted by permission of Houghton Mifflin Harcourt Publishing Company. All rights reserved.

Beacon Press for excerpt from *Man's Search for Meaning* by Viktor E. Frankl. Copyright © 1959, 1962, 1984, 1995 by Viktor E. Frankl. Reprinted by permission of Beacon Press. Boston.

PuddleDancer Press for excerpts from *Nonviolent Communication: A Language of Life* by Marshall B. Rosenberg. Copyright © 2003 by PuddleDancer Press.

DEDICATION

This book is dedicated to Paul Himmel, a social worker who helped me listen to myself in ways I didn't know I could.

It is also dedicated to the memory of my friends Joel Gallob and Anthony Milone, and to the memory of my parents, Abe and Mollie, for all the love and support they gave me.

Lastly, I dedicate this book to Werner Erhard who, by creating EST, inspired the work of Landmark Worldwide and the programs they offer, which showed me that all people can choose their lives.

GET YOUR BONUS EBOOK

"Step Out Of Your Comfort Zone and Watch Your Life Grow"

After reading this insightful, little eBook, you'll be able to:

- Discover the problems with the status quo
- Develop a mindset for change
- Make stepping out of your comfort zone a habit

For a free download of the eBook,
sign up for it here:

www.youcanchooseyourlife.com/step

CONTENTS

Introduction 1

PART I: **LOCKED INSIDE YOUR HEAD**

Chapter 1: From Internal Conversations to Life-Altering Choices—My Story 11

Chapter 2: Are You Choosing Your Life? 31

Chapter 3: Your Internal Conversations and Your Life 35

Chapter 4: Mental Prisons, Really? 45

Chapter 5: Stories and Judgments 51

Chapter 6: Choosing to Be a Victim 61

PART II: **FREEING YOURSELF FROM YOUR MENTAL PRISONS: WHAT YOU CAN DO**

Chapter 7: Why Being More Self-Aware Matters 71

Chapter 8: Taking Full Responsibility for Your Life 81

Chapter 9: Seven Keys to Unlock the Doors
of Your Mental Prisons 89
Chapter 10: Five Practices to Create a Life
You Love 99

PART III: GOING BEYOND THE FAMILIAR: WHAT'S POSSIBLE

Chapter 11: Creating from the Unknown 109
Chapter 12: Finding the Support You Need 115
Chapter 13: You Are The One 119
Chapter 14: Some Final Advice 127

Acknowledgments 131
Bibliography: Books and Films 137

INTRODUCTION

I wrote this self-help book because I know you can change your life by *choosing* your life. Yet, most of us don't. Most of us go along with the way things are, making adjustments whenever we can, wherever we can, while blaming ourselves, others, and the situations we're in for things not being the way we really want them to be.

This is very different from *choosing* your life. Choosing your life is an active process that requires you to be as aware, conscious, and responsible for the things you tell yourself and believe as you can possibly be.

And this is not something you do once and are done. No, choosing your life is something you must do again and again. But each time you choose it—that is, each time you take responsibility for your experience, whatever it may be—you come closer to living a life you love right now.

At the time I began writing this book I was participating in a course on personal growth and development offered by Landmark Education (now Landmark Worldwide). In that course I became acutely aware that I was not choosing my life. Instead, I was settling for the way things were.

My situation around my job was a perfect example of how I had settled. I was miserable at my job, yet I believed I couldn't find another job paying as much or more. And I wasn't making that much money to begin with. It was a customer service position in a call center. I had more than enough skills and education to qualify for a better paying and more interesting job, yet I believed this was as good as it was going to get, at least for a while. And I feared that if I quit, I wouldn't be able to pay my bills. The best way I can describe what I was experiencing at the time was that it felt like I was trapped in a mental prison. Only later did I realize it was a prison of my own making.

Having spent time in another kind of prison—the kind with cell doors that electronically lock, the kind a person can't get out of until the judge or the parole board gives the okay, the kind where correctional officers *shake down* your cell whenever they want, without any warning, throwing the few personal belongings you have all over the place as they search for contraband—I know how bad brick and mortar prisons can be. But I also know that our mental prisons are worse because, years later, when I wanted to leave that job I felt trapped in, I experienced being imprisoned again. And this time it was worse than being in a correctional institution because in the mental prison I was in I didn't know I'd ever get out.

I finally quit the job I had at the call center, but only after a good deal of suffering. And the only way I was able to quit was by recognizing that my fear about not being able to make it without that job was all in my head. What I learned from this experience is that our fears are continually stopping us from living lives we love. And most of our fears are in our head. But it's not just our fears that are stopping us. It's everything we tell ourselves and believe that we never question.

What Is In This Book

What's in this book is an argument that goes like this: We are all in mental prisons that are made up of our internal conversations. In order to choose your life, which you'll want to do so you can live a life you love, you have to take responsibility for your internal conversations. That's the whole book in a nutshell. But I have divided it into three parts: the first part looks at how our mental prisons are formed and how they operate, the second part focuses on what we can do to get out of them, and the third part explores what's possible for us when we do get out of them and step into the unknown.

Part I: LOCKED INSIDE YOUR HEAD begins with a chapter about my teenage years. I start with a story about this time in my life because it powerfully illustrates how my internal conversations shaped the choices I made. And hopefully it will help you see how your internal conversations shape your choices.

Even though I start with a chapter about my life and some of the choices I made in my youth, make no mistake about it: this book is about you and your choices. In the first part, you'll become aware of how your internal conversations have shaped and continue to shape the choices you make each and every day.

Part II: FREEING YOURSELF FROM YOUR MENTAL PRISONS: WHAT YOU CAN DO is about how becoming more aware and responsible for your internal conversations can help you free yourself from the mental prisons you're in. In this part, you'll find seven keys (metaphorical, of course) to unlock the doors of your mental prisons and five practices to help you live a life you love.

I do want to mention before I go any further that we are always going to be in different mental prisons—many of them at the same time. What this book will help you with is recognizing as many of them as you can, so that you can free yourself from each one you recognize. This doesn't mean you'll ever be able to recognize *all* of them or be free of *all* of them, but it does mean you'll be *a lot freer* than when you didn't know you were in any.

Part III: GOING BEYOND THE FAMILIAR: WHAT'S POSSIBLE is about what's possible when you are fully present in the moment and not stuck in the past. In this part, you'll find yourself in a discussion about what it means to create your life in the unknown rather than from your history. You'll see that like Neo, the main character in the movie *The Matrix*, you have powers you didn't know you had. In fact, when you believe in yourself, step outside your comfort zone, and get the support you need, all sorts of things will become possible for you that had not been possible before. You will realize that you really can choose your life and love the life you choose.

By the last page of this book, you will know beyond a shadow of a doubt that you have the power to choose your life the way it is as well as the way you want it to be. And you'll have the tools you'll need to be able to choose it both ways.

How to Get the Most from This Book

To get the most from this book, get yourself a notepad or create a folder on your desktop, laptop, or tablet, where you can answer the questions in the *Your Turn* sections that you'll find in almost every chapter. By answering these questions, you'll be engaged in an exploration about the choices you make beyond what reading alone can provide.

You might also consider starting a small group with three or four others who are also reading the book. If you do and your group gets together once or twice a month to discuss a new chapter each time, this book will come alive for you.

What I recommend is that you go through the book first by yourself and then a second time with the people in your group. Read it through the first time without answering the questions. Then, after your group is formed, go through the book again answering the questions and sharing your answers with the people in your group. I also recommend that you put your answers in writing. This way, not only will you be able to share what you've written with others, but you'll be able to reflect on what you've written any time you want.

If you are not going to participate in a group, then of course, answer the questions as soon as you come upon them. There is no right way to go through this book. But do answer the questions. And have fun discovering whatever you discover. After all, this is *your* journey. You might as well enjoy the ride.

And if you find that you're resonating with what's in these pages, please go to *www.YouCanChooseYourLife.com* for a free gift and more.

PART I

LOCKED INSIDE YOUR HEAD

CHAPTER 1

FROM INTERNAL CONVERSATIONS TO LIFE-ALTERING CHOICES— MY STORY

When I was a teenager, I had conversations going on in my head that made me think of myself as a loser. I wasn't good at sports or school; therefore, I thought the only way I could prove my self-worth was by doing things that everyone else was afraid of doing. So I did those things in spite of the fact that some of them involved breaking the law. This led me down a path of juvenile delinquency.

Yet, at the time, I had no idea that I had chosen to go down this path or any path for that matter. Nor did I know that the choices I was making had anything to do with the conversations in my head or that I even had conversations in my head. But I did. And the conversations I was listening to in my head had everything to do with the choices I was making.

Becoming a Juvenile Delinquent: A Story

When I was 14, I had these friends who were noticeably wealthier than I was. Their families were not only wealthier than mine, but these friends were also more accomplished than me in many ways. For example, a number of them played musical instruments, and I did not. They also played softball, which I tried to play but was never good at. In addition, they liked going to school dances, and I couldn't dance to save my life. But the real kicker was that most of them did well in school, which was the last thing I thought I'd ever do well in.

Still, we hung out together with me trying my best to keep up with them, but I knew that I'd never be as confident and accomplished as they were. As far as I was concerned, these kids were much more together and talented than I would ever be. So after trying to fit in with them for about a year, I decided it was time to look for other friends—kids who were more on my level.

I thought I'd found them in Ricky and Louis (not their real names), two boys who lived in the same neighborhood I did, just a few blocks from my house. Like me, Ricky and Louis didn't play softball, go to school dances, or get good grades. In fact, all they seemed to care about was riding their sharp-looking bicycles with banana seats and motorcycle handle bars.

In almost every way, these boys challenged how I was taught teenagers should be. For example, they smoked cigarettes, drank alcohol, and stayed out until the early hours of the morning, even on school nights. In fact, Ricky, who was 16, had dropped out of high school; and Louis, who was 14, my age at the time, hardly went to any of his junior high classes. Even though I didn't do any of the things they did when I first met them, I began doing everything they did and more within a short period of time. I did what they did because I wanted to fit in. I thought Ricky and Louis were cool, and I wanted to be like them instead of the shy, obedient, and insecure boy I thought of myself as.

Both Ricky and Louis seemed more interested in living life on their own terms than in anything else. They were being how I only wished I could be. They were living on the edge—on the dangerous side of life. They exemplified the free spirit I yearned to have, and they didn't take orders from anyone. While I was in school, doing what I was supposed to, they were hanging out, doing what they wanted. I was fascinated by their *you-*

can't-tell-me-what-to-do attitude. And I was looking for friends who I knew other kids wouldn't mess with and who'd accept me as I was. I thought Ricky and Louis fitted the bill, so I chose to hang out with them. But it didn't occur like a choice at all. It just seemed like something I wanted to do.

But whether I was or wasn't aware of it, I was making choices when I was a teenager. And many of the choices I was making went against everything I had been taught. For example, I didn't have to start smoking cigarettes and drinking alcohol when I was 14, and stealing people's bicycles and cars a year after that. Nor did I have to start hanging out with Ricky and Louis, two boys that my parents didn't want me around. But I did those things because I chose to.

I later saw that I made a lot of choices when I was a teenager just to fit in. I believed that the only way I could fit in was by doing things that would make me seem fearless and cool, even though I really wasn't. So I did things I was afraid of doing just to belong.

I was definitely not an angel. But neither was I a really bad kid. I had grown up with two working class parents, undergone the traditional coming-of-age ceremony known in my Jewish tradition as a bar mitzvah, and followed my parents' rules—at least until I started hanging out with Ricky and Louis. Even though I was not an angel, I never intentionally did anything to hurt anyone who hadn't hurt me first.

Aware of it or not though, my choices *were* hurting people. For instance, it must have hurt my father when he discovered his candy store had been broken into with his own key—the one he had right up until the time he went to bed. I lifted the key out of his pants pocket while he was asleep. When he found out about the burglary the next day and discovered his key missing, he must have put the two together. Not surprisingly, he asked me if I had any knowledge about the break in. I lied even though I'm sure he knew I was involved. That must have hurt.

I imagine the owners of the bicycles and cars I stole were also hurt when they discovered their property missing. Skipping classes as much as I did must have hurt my teachers too, not to mention how it hurt my own education. I know I hurt my parents by not listening to them. Every time my mother urged me to stop hanging out with Ricky and Louis, I ignored her. And whenever my father asked me to do a chore, I usually ignored him too. My disobedient behavior must have hurt both my parents. It must also have hurt my two younger sisters, because I was not a good role model for them.

Whether I was or wasn't aware of it, I was making choices during my teenage years. And many of them were hurting people—more people than I care to admit.

When I was 16, I chose to steal a 1964 Chevy Impala because I wanted its mag wheels for my car. I knew the owner of the car would have to get new wheels to replace the ones I stole, but I believed his insurance would reimburse him for that. So it didn't seem like a big deal to me to steal the Chevy for its wheels. However, what initially didn't seem like a big deal ended up being a very big deal, because the night I stole the Chevy Impala I was stopped by the police and a deadly police chase ensued.

I stole the car because I didn't have enough money to buy the mag wheels myself. I was listening to a conversation in my head that told me I'd never get those wheels if I had to wait until I could buy them. I believed it would have taken me at least a year, maybe two, to have saved enough. And that seemed too long to wait. Plus, I didn't think I had to wait, as I had watched Ricky steal other people's cars to take parts off of them for his own car. I didn't see why I couldn't do the same.

I was very proud to be driving around in my Pontiac GTO—the family car that Dad let me pick out and which I treated as mine. It was a sharp looking car. And I knew it would look even sharper by putting mag wheels on it, so I was determined to get those wheels.

And I found the ones I wanted on a Chevy Impala in Riverdale, New York, that was parked on the same street almost every night. With Ricky's help, I planned to break into the car, drive it to a deserted area, remove its wheels and, after things had died down, put them on the GTO.

On the night I decided to steal the Impala, everything went as planned—at least initially. I broke into the car a little after midnight. Ricky hot-wired it in less than three minutes. And in less than six minutes, I was driving the car away. In twenty-five minutes, we were both in Greenburg, New York, at the rendezvous spot where we had agreed to meet—me in the Impala and Ricky in the GTO. Everything was going along perfectly.

There was just one problem. When we got to the clearing in the woods where we were going to remove the wheels, there were three cars already there. This was a bit unusual since it was one o'clock in the morning on a weekday night. As soon as I got closer, I realized the situation was even worse. The three cars were all police cars.

In spite of the fact that I was terrified after realizing that I had fallen into some type of trap, I decided my best strategy was to drive away slowly and cautiously, so as not to draw any unnecessary attention to myself or to Ricky, wherever he might be. And that's what I did.

But I must have been followed because, as soon as I was out of the wooded area and on a paved street, I heard the sharp, loud blast of a police siren followed by red and white, flashing roof lights that illuminated the pitch-black sky.

I knew what I was supposed to do next, so I pulled off to the side of the road as was expected of me and waited. But as I thought about what, in all likelihood, was going to happen—that I'd be arrested, convicted, and sent away to one of those places in upstate New York that I had heard so many terrible things about, maybe for a year, maybe two, for grand larceny auto—it occurred to me that I might be able to avoid all that.

I certainly didn't want to wait to discover what life was like in one of those reformatories, where boys are forced to be bedfellows with other bigger boys and lots of kids come out as hardened criminals. I didn't want that to happen to me. But I was sure it would if I got arrested because I was already on probation for having stolen another car.

I was sweating profusely as I waited for the police officer to come over to the Chevy and ask for the license and registration I didn't have. I did have a learner's permit, but that meant I needed a licensed driver in the car with me at all times. Of course, I didn't have one. I also had no idea where the registration for the stolen car was. Even if it was somewhere inside, it would be in another person's name, so that wouldn't help.

I kept thinking of what I could do to get out of the situation I was in, and then it hit me: I could take off! Every cell in my body began screaming *Take off while you still can!* I knew I needed a little lead time, so I waited for the police officer to open his car door and start walking in my direction. A second passed. Then another. And finally, I heard the officer's car door open and the crunch of gravel under his boots as he took his first steps towards the Chevy. Without a second to waste, I put the car in gear and pressed down as hard as I could on the gas pedal. The Impala bolted forward, kicking up gravel as it sped away.

Trying to get away from the police in a stolen car is a crazy thing to do, but I *chose* to do it. Or did I? When we do things because we feel we have to is that really making a choice? At the time, I was terrified and was sure that if I didn't get away I would be sent away. Taking off seemed like the only thing I could do to remain free.

But I did have other choices. For instance, I could have chosen to wait until the police officer came over to the Impala, and then I could have had a conversation with him. During the conversation, I could have told the officer that I knew I was driving with a learner's permit, but that my father let me take the car out anyway. I could have also told the officer that I had left the registration for the Chevy at home and asked him if he would give me a break this one time. Another choice I had was to tell the officer the truth and ask for mercy. I *did* have other choices. However, based on the conversations I was having with myself, I didn't. I had convinced myself that if I didn't take off, I'd be arrested and sent away. And since I didn't want that to happen, I pressed my foot down on the gas pedal like a man possessed.

The problem with having to make choices when we're under pressure is that we almost always make the wrong choice. We usually go along with the first thing we tell ourselves without thinking things through. During these times, our ability to look at and understand the big picture is compromised by the immediacy of the moment.

That's what happened when I stepped on the gas pedal that early October morning: my ability to look at the big picture and consider the consequences of my actions had completely disappeared. There were better choices I could have made; but because I was listening to a conversation in my head that told me I'd be locked up and sent away if I didn't get away, I made the only choice that seemed to offer any possibility of freedom at the time. Looking back on it now, I am clear it was the worst choice I could have made.

When I chose to step on the gas pedal that early October morning, there were so many things I had not considered. For example, I didn't consider that the officer who had pulled me over would call other police cars to join in a high-speed chase. Nor did I consider that there were twenty miles of expressway I'd have to travel before arriving home. I also didn't imagine I'd have to drive at speeds of over 100 miles per hour to stay ahead of the police, who would be pursuing me with their sirens blaring, red and white roof-lights flashing, and even a few gunshots being fired by one or two officers who'd want to put a little fear in my heart. There was a lot I had not considered when I stepped on the gas pedal that early October morning when I was sixteen.

Once on the expressway, my speedometer registered 115 miles per hour. I had to go that fast to stay ahead of the police who were in close pursuit. I also had to do some dangerous maneuvering, like crossing over the expressway divide to avoid crashing into two police cars that had entered the expressway in front of me in an attempt to block my way.

I was lucky that I didn't have a head-on collision when I was travelling south on the northbound lanes of the Major Deegan Expressway. I believe the only reason I didn't have one was because it was so early in the morning and there weren't that many cars on the road yet. Had there been more, I doubt I would have survived.

As soon I got ahead of the two police cars that had tried to block my way, I was able to cross back over the expressway, going in the same direction as traffic again. It was a harrowing experience. My adrenalin was pumping the whole time, and I felt like I was driving for my life. Of course, I was.

After another ten minutes on the expressway with the police still in close pursuit, I arrived at the outskirts of my neighborhood. If I was going to exit, I knew this was the time to do it. My plan was to follow the local, city streets to within a few blocks of my house, ditch the stolen car, and then run the rest of the way home on foot. When I got home, I was going to climb back into my bedroom through the same window I had climbed out.

But as soon as the car was on the exit ramp, I realized that to get home I'd have to make a ninety degree turn at the intersection I was approaching, and I couldn't make that turn at the speed I was going. If I tried, I was certain the car would flip over with me inside it. And I couldn't slow down very much either, because there was no time. So I decided to do the only thing I could do, which was to go straight through the intersection and get back on the expressway. I didn't want to do that, but I didn't think I had any other choice—certainly no other survivable one.

And then the light changed at the intersection from green to red. And a Ford Fairlane pulled into the middle. I couldn't believe it. The driver of the car had to have seen my car speeding towards the intersection. He had to have heard the sounds of sirens and seen the flashing lights of the police cars getting brighter and brighter the closer they came. But his car remained stationary. And I was coming straight towards it. I pressed down as hard as I could on the brake pedal and leaned on the horn until it let out a continuous wail. But it was too late.

I awoke to a voice shouting, "Get out with your hands up." I didn't know where the voice was coming from or who it was directed at. All I knew was that I was in pain and could hardly move.

Within seconds I felt someone tugging on my clothes. It was the police officer who had been shouting. He was trying to pull me out of the Impala. But it was difficult as the driver's door wouldn't budge. When the officer finally got me out, he told me in a very angry voice to stand where I was, completely oblivious to the fact that I was scrunched over in pain.

And more like a statement rather than a question, he belted out in a loud voice, "You want to see what you've done?" He then told me to look in the direction of a stretcher that was being wheeled into the back of a vehicle not far from where we were standing. I looked, but I wasn't sure what I was looking at. In addition to having a case of temporary amnesia, I was also in shock, so things weren't making a whole lot of sense to me. I didn't know where I was or how I had gotten to this place. However, I do remember seeing a white sheet on the stretcher that was covering something. I learned later that under that white sheet was the body of the man I had killed. I was devastated.

I had never intended anything like this to happen. I had never planned to hurt anyone.

What Happened Next

As a consequence of the choices I made that mournful Columbus Day, the driver of the car I hit died, his one and only passenger was seriously injured, and I was sentenced to four years behind bars. My sentence was later reduced to three years because my father wrote a letter to the judge, pleading for leniency by making the case that his son had never been involved in a violent crime before.

I was lucky—lucky to have gotten my sentence reduced and lucky to have come out of the car crash alive. Nevertheless, I was also scared, angry, and confused because I was going to be spending time behind bars for something I had never intended to happen. And I was sure that none of what happened would have happened had the police not chosen to pursue me. Had they not gone after me, I am sure I would have never been driving at the speeds I was driving, nor would I have crashed into another vehicle, killing a man and injuring his passenger. Because of what happened that morning many years ago, I am very much against police chases to this day.

Yet I do know that none of what happened would have happened if I hadn't set everything in motion by stealing the Impala in the first place. But even before that—actually, many years before it—I was listening to conversations in my head that told me I'd have to prove my self-worth to others if I wanted to be accepted by them. And I needed to be accepted by them because I didn't accept myself.

Today, I can see that everything that led up to my stealing the Impala and getting into a fatal car crash was tied to conversations I was listening to in my head, which started long before I ever met Ricky and Louis, and long before I ever stole anything.

Listening for Opportunities

Those internal conversations I was listening to in my head during my teenage years were running my life, but I was determined that I was not going to let them *ruin* my life—certainly not any more than they already had.

So even though I had been sentenced to three years behind bars and had started serving my time, I decided to turn my life around. I knew I couldn't change the past, but I believed I could change my future. And I began listening for opportunities to do that.

Two big opportunities that I was able to take advantage of while I was incarcerated were being able to go to the school they had at Rikers Island to get my GED and being able to meet regularly with a social worker who was doing a year-long internship at the prison.

Initially, I wasn't sure I wanted to do either of those things. It might be obvious why I didn't want to go to the school they had at Rikers Island. Since one of my internal conversations had me convinced that I was not smart, I knew succeeding in school would be a huge challenge for me. I had doubts about whether I would be able to pass any of the tests I needed to take to get my GED certificate. And I wasn't big on meeting with a social worker either, because I didn't see myself as a particularly trusting person. It was hard for me to imagine sharing my private thoughts with anyone—no less a stranger. I feared that the social worker would tell the prison authorities everything I told him in confidence.

Clearly, my internal conversations were doing their best to stop me from recognizing the two opportunities before me as opportunities. However, I did have a dream for the future, and I believed in that dream. To achieve my dream I knew that I would have to be educated, so I could write an intelligent book that people would want to read, and I'd have to be comfortable with who I was since I'd be in the spotlight from time to time, having to talk about the books I'd written, as well as about myself. Based on my dream to become a successful, published author, going to school to get my GED and having regular meetings with a social worker seemed like two actions I needed to take.

Nevertheless, my internal conversations were doing everything they could to stop me. Fortunately, they didn't win out. My dream did. In the end, not only did I go to the school they had at Rikers Island and pass all the tests I needed to pass to get my GED certificate, but I also got one of the highest scores of anyone who had ever taken those tests at Rikers Island since the place had opened. And meeting regularly with Mr. Himmel, the social worker, helped me realize that not only was I a person who was worthy of other people's time and attention, but that I could trust others and others could trust me too.

Taking advantage of both of these opportunities that were made available to me while I was incarcerated was life-changing. It showed me that I really *could* change the direction my life was heading and accomplish things I had no idea I could.

After I was released, I registered at Lehman College in Bronx, New York. And after two semesters there, I was put on the Dean's List for academic excellence. And I stayed on the Dean's List until the end of my studies.

In three and a half years, I had a bachelor degree and graduated college with honors. Then I went on to get a Master of Arts in Creative Writing and another Master of Arts in Criminal Justice. These were all things I *chose* to do and did—me, a former juvenile delinquent and a high school dropout!

I also promised myself that I would never be incarcerated again, and I kept that promise too. When I got out of Rikers Island and Ossining Correctional Facility, I disassociated myself from my former friends—specifically Ricky and Louis—and I began to make new friends at the college I was attending. As you can see from reading this book, I also became the published author I had always wanted to be. The fact is I changed the direction my life was heading. And you can too.

I share this story with you because *I believe we can all change the direction in which our lives are heading if we're committed to doing that.* And it doesn't matter what's happened in the past. What matters is the future you are choosing to create and your willingness to do the work to create it.

CHAPTER 2

ARE YOU CHOOSING YOUR LIFE?

Well, are you? You make hundreds of choices every day. You choose the time you go to sleep and the time you wake up; to brush your teeth in the morning, brush them at night, or not brush them at all; what you eat and at what time, or whether to skip meals altogether.

On a larger scale, you choose where you live: in the city, the country, by the ocean or in the mountains. You choose whether to marry, date, or stay single, and if you live in a house, an apartment, a hotel, or have some other living arrangement. You also choose what you do for a living or if you work for a living at all. The fact is you are making choices all the time. You will make so many choices over the course of your life that you couldn't possibly count them all.

In spite of all of the choices you make however, you still probably don't have the experience that you are *choosing* your life. Instead, if you're like most of us, you probably believe that your parents, circumstances, fate, or biology—or all four—are responsible for the person you are today. These people and things have certainly left their mark on you, but you are a lot more responsible for choosing your life than you realize.

A Special Kind of Choice

Although this book is about choice, it's not about choice in the way we most often think about it: *the red car* or *the blue one, work hard and earn the promotion* or *spend more time at home with the loved ones*. Rather, it's about choice as the profoundly liberating capacity that we as human beings have to choose our experience of life at every moment.

Viktor Frankl, who was a prisoner in a Nazi concentration camp during World War II, refers to this kind of choice in his well-known book, *Man's Search for Meaning,* when he writes:

> We who lived in concentration camps can remember the men who walked through the huts comforting others, giving away their last piece of bread. They may have been few in number, but they offer sufficient proof that everything can be taken from a man but one thing: the last of the human freedoms—to choose one's attitude in any given set of circumstances, to choose one's own way.

From reading Frankl's words, it is clear that some of the men imprisoned chose not to be robbed of their inner-freedom. Instead they chose to maintain their humanity even when it meant giving away their last piece of bread.

What Frankl witnessed is proof that we can all choose our lives, no matter what situation we are in. And when we do, we get to say what our experience of life is instead of having others tell us what it should be.

Yet a number of us believe that we have little to no choice when it comes to our experience of life. You may be one of them.

Think back to yesterday and describe what it was like for you. Was it a challenging day, a carefree day, a busy day? Let's say it was a challenging day. When you think back to it, do you go over all the things that happened that made it seem challenging—things that you believed you could do nothing about? But was it the events that made it seem challenging? Or was it how you *chose* to interpret those events?

Do You Choose Your Life?

Of course, you do! In fact, you are choosing it all the time. The problem is that you're not aware you are. And since you're not aware you are, it may not seem like you're choosing your life at all. You may actually feel like a victim some of the time. Now, you may not want to acknowledge that, but that's how a lot of us feel when things don't go our way and when we think we have no control over what's happening.

But we do have a choice regarding how we're going to respond to things that happen. We actually have a lot more choices in this arena than most of us realize.

So the answer to the question *Do You Choose Your Life?* is you do. You choose your life by choosing your experience of life. And you're choosing your experience all the time, even when you are not aware you are.

That's where this book comes in. One of its aims is to show you how you can become more aware of the choices you're making, so you don't have to continue making the same choices that have been producing the same results.

CHAPTER 3

YOUR INTERNAL CONVERSATIONS AND YOUR LIFE

We all have internal conversations. But some of them are buried so deep in our unconscious that we rarely hear them. For this reason, it doesn't seem like we're talking to ourselves at all, even though we are. And we do it without even opening our mouths!

Yes, there are things you are telling yourself 24/7. And no, you're not crazy! Everyone does this. We are telling ourselves different things all the time. It's as if we're having a series of internal conversations with ourselves when no one else is around. And we are! We're even having them when others are around.

There are questions we ask ourselves (*Did I do that right?*), criticisms we have of ourselves (*Darn, I missed that one!*), judgments we make about others (*His tie doesn't go with his shirt.*), responses to situations (*That looks scary.*), even commands we give ourselves (*Stop being so nice all the time!*), and inquiries we have about almost everything (*I wonder what she meant by that?*).

Sound familiar?

Here's something you may not know: these internal conversations you're having with yourself make up the contents of your mental prisons. As much as they allow you to experience the many things you do experience, they stop you from experiencing the many things you don't experience, and may never experience, if you keep on listening to the same internal conversations over and over again.

Listen Right Now

If you want to hear a few of your own internal conversations right now, you can. All you have to do is put down this book, find a quiet and comfortable place to sit, and close your eyes. For the next three to five minutes, try clearing your mind of everything. And when you are done sitting in silence, ask yourself what you heard.

Assuming you're back from sitting in silence, what did you hear? Did you hear the sounds of people talking around you or birds chirping outside? If it was quiet enough, perhaps you heard some of your own thoughts. Perhaps you heard yourself say to yourself, *I don't know why I'm doing this,* or *I have no idea what this author expects me to hear.*

Whatever you heard—whether it seemed to come from outside yourself or from inside your own head—you put what you heard into language and gave it meaning. And the meaning you gave to what you heard is now part of your internal conversations.

Of course, you may refer to what I'm calling internal conversations as thoughts, beliefs, judgments, or stories. They are all of this and more. But I'm calling them internal conversations here because they are the things we tell ourselves and respond to.

Where Our Internal Conversations Come From

Our internal conversations come from many different sources. Some of them come from our primary caregivers, extended family members, friends, teachers, and neighbors. Others come from the books, magazines, and blogs we read; and the television shows, movies, plays, and news programs we watch. Then there are the radio shows, speeches, debates, and music lyrics we listen to. And let's not forget the neighborhoods where we were raised, the countries we call home, and the religions and cultures we were brought up in. We get our internal conversations from all these sources and more.

The conversations we internalize the most, however, come from our parents or whoever raised us. A good example of one of these conversations is the one we have about marriage. Most of us know before we're even teenagers the age our parents expect us to be married by, the type of bride or groom our parents expect us to marry, as well as the kind of ceremony they'd like us to have.

My friend Golam certainly knew these things. When I met him he was living in the U.S. and in a Ph.D. program at the University of Texas in Dallas, where I was also attending. I remember one day he got a call from one of his younger brothers telling him that there was a woman his brother wanted to marry, but he wouldn't marry her until Golam, the eldest brother, got married first.

Not long after this call—even though Golam was enjoying life in Texas and was hoping to find a way to stay in the U.S. after he got his Ph.D.—he was soon on a plane back to Bangladesh to marry a woman who had been selected for him by his mother. And he never returned to the U.S. to finish his Ph.D. or settle down.

I share this this story with you because it illustrates the power that our internal conversations have over us. In this example, Golam inherited a conversation about the eldest son needing to marry before his younger siblings and another one about having one's bride selected by one's parents. And he honored both of them. As a result of doing so, he ended up changing his plans for the future entirely. Instead of finishing his Ph.D. and settling down in the U.S., he returned to Bangladesh and started a family there.

It may not sound like a big deal that Golam did what he did, but it is! And he did it based on conversations he had inherited—conversations that eventually became his own.

There's nothing unusual about this. But a lot of us don't realize that these conversations, which are passed down to us and which we internalize, shape our lives. Over time they become our own guiding directives, whether we're conscious of following them or not.

YOUR TURN—

Take a few minutes now to explore one of your own internal conversations. If you're not yet sure about the term "internal conversation," just focus on one of your beliefs. For example, you might look at one of your beliefs about marriage, money, religion, or family. In your notebook or on your computer, write down how you first acquired this belief and why you still adhere to it today. If you no longer adhere to it, explain what changed.

Here are some additional questions to help you go deeper into this inquiry:

How does the belief you identified influence the way you think about yourself and relate to others? Does it affect how generous or prudent you are? Does it have you treat certain people differently than you treat others?

After you've written down your answers to these questions, share what you've written with the people in your group. If you're not in a group, share your answers to these and all the Your Turn questions that follow with at least one person you know and trust.

A Disempowering Conversation I Inherited

Although different from the conversation that Golam inherited about the eldest son needing to marry before his younger brothers, I'd like to share a conversation I inherited when I was young. This one is about being stupid. It was passed down to me from people I respected and looked up to, including my father, teachers, and friends.

In fact, I can still remember my dad saying to me on multiple occasions, *"What do you know? You're only a child!"* Whenever my dad said this, and it was often, I got the message: *I didn't know much.*

I got a similar message from my teachers without them having to say a word to me. It was obvious from my report card grades and how my teachers responded to me in class that they didn't think I was very smart. It seemed that whenever I would raise my hand to answer one of their questions in class, they would not call on me. It is true that one time when I didn't know the correct answer to one of my teacher's questions, I raised my hand to give a silly answer instead. After that I don't think I was ever called on again. It didn't matter that I would be the only kid in class with his hand raised. *What did I know? Clearly, not much!*

I also got a similar message from my friends. Every time I didn't understand something they said or did, they would break out laughing.

Based on what my father, teachers, and friends said and did, I became convinced that I was not intelligent and never would be. It is no wonder that I didn't put much effort into school and cut classes in junior high and high school until I finally quit. I had completely bought into the conversation that I was stupid. And I had all the evidence I needed to support it.

YOUR TURN—

Think about an internal conversation you have about yourself that holds you back in some area of your life. It can be the conversation you have already started to explore or a new one. Write down how you think you acquired this conversation and how it holds you back in your life. Also write down the evidence you use to support this belief you have about yourself. When your group meets, share with them what you've written.

Disempowering Conversations

As you can see, there are a number of problems associated with growing up on a diet of disempowering conversations. But the main one is that these conversations, which we internalize, can limit what's possible for us.

In my case, if it hadn't been for people who believed in me, like Mr. Himmel, my social worker at Rikers Island; Mr. Greenhouse, the English teacher who made certain my poems were published in the high school yearbook; and Mr. Seeman, a high school counselor who used his own time after class to talk to me, I might have never realized that there was another path I could take besides the one I was on. And I doubt I would have accomplished the many things I did when I was incarcerated and after I was released.

The support I received from others was life-saving. But it wasn't the support by itself that made the difference. It was the support along with my willingness to *accept* it and do whatever I could to live into an imagined future rather than stay stuck in disempowering conversations from my past.

Only you know what it will take for you to stop listening to the disempowering conversations that hold you back in life. But one thing is certain: until you are willing to acknowledge that you are listening to disempowering conversations that hold you back, you'll continue listening to them and they'll continue holding you back. They'll also continue influencing everything you think, say, and do—shaping not only the way you feel about yourself, but also how you feel about others and even how others feel about you.

YOUR TURN—

Write about one or two people who have helped you out when you were going through difficult times. Describe how this person or these people supported you or continue to support you during difficult times. Also write about what you've done yourself to help you get through difficult times. Then share what you've written with the people in your group when you next meet.

CHAPTER 4

MENTAL PRISONS, REALLY?

Let's assume that there are no bars on the doors or windows of your home—certainly none you can't open—and that you are free to come and go when you want and say and do almost anything you want as long as you pay your taxes, don't physically hurt others, and don't break any laws. Based on this, it seems you have a lot of freedom, doesn't it?

And you do!

If you are living in a Western-style democracy, you can practice any religion you want, criticize the government when you have a complaint, and even get laws passed to suit your needs.

In spite of all this freedom, however, you're still trapped inside a mental prison—actually, many of them. And each one you're in dictates how life occurs to you all the time.

Why Mental Prisons?

Because we're locked inside our head. Whether we realize it or not, we're locked inside the thoughts, beliefs, stories, and opinions that make us who we are. Of course, we need those thoughts, beliefs, stories, and opinions, so we know who we are and have a sense of the world we're dealing with. But they also limit us, especially when they stop us from entertaining thoughts, beliefs, stories, and opinions that are different from our own. When they do, we stay stuck with what we got and what we know. We stay locked into relating to life one particular way when there are thousands of ways to relate to it.

So the answer to the question *Why Mental Prisons* is that it's an excellent metaphor to help us understand why we are stuck where we are in life and how recognizing our internal conversations can help us become unstuck. Using this metaphor enables us to see that we have something to do with the way we show up in the world and the way the world shows up to us. Of course, as soon as we see this, we can do something about it. We can change how we show up in the world and how the world shows up to us. If we know we're in mental prisons, we can work on getting ourselves out of them, so we can enjoy more peace, freedom, and happiness in our lives.

Another reason to use this metaphor is that it has us work on ourselves. It takes the focus away from external things and puts the focus on us. Instead of blaming others or blaming our circumstances or even blaming ourselves, we can focus on understanding our part in having life show up the way it does for us.

Of course, we can continue to blame others. No one is saying that others haven't done their part in having our lives show up the way they do. But blaming anyone doesn't help us understand ourselves any better, nor does it help us recognize the different mental prisons we're in, so we can get out of them.

Why Many of Them?

Because there are many of them! We are in many different mental prisons all the time, and at the same time.

In the introduction, I shared about feeling imprisoned when I was at a job I didn't think I could leave. That was one mental prison I was in. During the same period of time, I was in another mental prison that had me convinced that the job I had was not fulfilling. In addition to that mental prison, I was in a third mental prison that had me believing I couldn't find another job paying as much or more. I was also feeling depressed because I wasn't pursuing my dream to become the published author I always wanted to be.

These were all different mental prisons I was in at the same time. And they are not even half of the ones I was in then. They're just the ones I remember being in that had to do with a job I didn't like. But the cause of my unhappiness was not so much with the job as it was with my stories and beliefs about the job.

So, again, the answer to *Why Many of Them* is because we are in many of them. And the more of them that we recognize we're in, the more of them we can get out of. The good news is that we only have to start by getting out of one. But once we can get out of one, it will not be long before we try to get out of another and then another one after that. There is nothing like experiencing more peace, freedom, and happiness in our lives. And that's what you'll experience as soon as you start freeing yourself from the mental prisons you're in.

Problems with Using this Metaphor

It would be not be truthful to say that there aren't problems with using this metaphor. There definitely are. The first and biggest one is that most of us don't see ourselves as being locked inside our head at all. We may recognize that our thoughts, beliefs, stories, and opinions stop us from entertaining thoughts, beliefs, stories, and opinions that are contrary to our own. But we don't usually see this as a problem. And we certainly don't see it as imprisoning.

Another problem with using this metaphor is that it means we've got work to do on ourselves. We have to figure out which mental prisons we're in and how to get out of them. I wrote this book to help with that. But it's still going to require time and effort. And you may not want to do the work.

Many people don't even know where to begin. You may be one of them. Or you may feel like you already have enough work to do in your life, starting with your forty-hour a week job, which, of course, must come first. But working on yourself has to come right after that.

It is that important—in many ways even more important than changing your circumstances. Actually, working on yourself will help you change your circumstances because it has the potential to change how you relate to everything. Still, a lot of people may not see the value of this. They may not believe they can change who they are even though our lives are changing all the time.

So these are some of the problems that come with using this metaphor. And there are more. But they can all be overcome and have to be if you intend to use this metaphor as a tool to help you choose your life. If you don't recognize the problems that come with using this metaphor of a mental prison, they'll stop you before you even attempt to step foot outside your cell door.

YOUR TURN—

Examine another area of your life where you feel stuck or unhappy. It could be around your career, job, marriage, family, health, or anything else. Write down why you feel stuck or unhappy in this area of your life and explore how using this metaphor of a mental prison can be helpful.

If you don't feel stuck or unhappy in any area of your life, write about what would make you feel happier than you already are. When you're done, share what you've written with the people in your group.

CHAPTER 5

STORIES AND JUDGMENTS

As human beings, one way we make sense of reality is by creating stories. We have stories about who we are and how we got to be the way we are. We also have stories about who other people are and how they got to be the way they are. We even have stories about the world and why it is the way it is. We have stories about everything and everyone. There's almost nothing that we don't have stories about.

And our stories are part of our internal conversations. However, they are much more elaborate than any of the one sentence statements we say to ourselves throughout the day. Our stories have a beginning, middle, and an ending. They also have a judgment at their core, which is supported by evidence that seems hard to refute.

Where Our Stories Come From

Some of our stories we inherit, and others we make up. But whether we inherit them or make them up, we relate to our stories as *the truth*. In fact, what I'm calling stories here may not occur like stories at all to you, because to you they are the truth.

But our stories are, and will forever be, only stories. They are based on things that have happened and our interpretation of those things. It's important that we recognize this: that it's never the things that have happened by themselves that give us our stories. It's always the things that have happened *along with our interpretation* of those things.

Uncovering a Story That Was Imprisoning Me

In 1996, when I was participating in a three-day course on personal growth and development called the Landmark Forum, I discovered that I had more than a few stories about my life. Before I did the course, I didn't know I had any. As far as I was concerned what I thought was true about me was true.

For example, I was sure I was a bad person. Even though I did my best to appear like everyone else, deep inside I knew I was different. Still, I was surprised to find myself trembling when I shared with the other participants in the Landmark Forum about what had happened the night I stole the Chevy Impala.

What I came to understand in that course was that I was trembling not because of what had happened, but because of what I had made it mean: that I was a terrible person who should be ashamed to be alive.

In the Landmark Forum, I learned that we all make up stories about things that happen. And our stories are composed of two things: what happened and what we make it mean. We end up putting the two together, relating to the whole thing as the truth. But our stories are never the truth because a part of them is nothing but interpretation and judgment.

For example, in my case, what happened when I was 16 was that I stole a car, got into a police chase, hit another car in which one person died and another person was injured. That's what happened. What I made it mean was that I was a terrible person who should be ashamed to be alive. That was my interpretation.

But I was never a terrible person in spite of the fact I thought of myself that way for years. It wasn't until I did the Landmark Forum that I was able to see that I had created a story about myself that was based on my interpretation of what happened the night I got into the fatal car crash.

Certainly, I wish what had happened had never happened. I am sorry that I caused as much pain and suffering as I did. But that doesn't mean I should go through life ashamed to be alive.

Recognizing this was life-changing for me. It meant I didn't have to be a victim anymore. I could own my past without having to hide from it. Of course, what happened during those years is not something I want everyone to know about. But what happened, happened. I can choose to learn and grow from the experience to become a better person as a result of it, or I can choose to be resentful and stay a victim for the rest of my life. This is a choice I get to to make. And it's a choice we all get to make when we recognize our stories are imprisoning us. Of course, we first must recognize our stories as stories, which is not easy to do since most of us have been relating to them as the truth for years.

But it's essential that we do recognize our stories as stories if we want to get out of the mental prisons we're in and start living lives we love.

YOUR TURN—

Think of something significant that happened in your life that you felt was diminishing or demeaning. What happened and what did you make it mean? First, write down what happened. Then on a separate sheet of paper write down what you made it mean. After you've done this, consider the affect that your story has had on your life and write that down too. And if you're seeing your story as a story for the first time, write down what it's like recognizing that it's not the truth. When the people in your group meet share with them what you've written.

Facing Your Sentence

In another Landmark course, I discovered that not only did I have a story about the person I believed I was, but that I had sentenced myself to the life I had based on my story.

During that course, it became clear to me that I had sentenced myself to a life of suffering and struggle because of my belief that I was this terrible person who should be ashamed to be alive.

If you had asked me before I took the course, however, if I had sentenced myself to a life of suffering and struggle, I would have said, "You've got to be kidding. Why would anyone in his right mind do that to himself?" But now, I see that we *all* sentence ourselves to the lives we're living, based on the stories we tell ourselves and believe about ourselves.

Your Story and Your Sentence

If you have a story about being a bad person like I did, for example, it makes sense that you would sentence yourself to a life of suffering and struggle, like I did, in order to punish yourself for being bad.

Similarly, if you have a story about being overweight, it makes sense that you would sentence yourself to feeling guilty every time you ate foods that you knew you shouldn't. And if you have a story about being a loner, it makes sense you would sentence yourself to being uncomfortable and feeling out of place every time you were around other people.

The point is that we all sentence ourselves based on the stories we tell ourselves about ourselves. And our sentences show up in the kind of lives we live. Below is a prose poem, written by Russell Edson that illustrates this point in a very unique way.

The Judgment

A man dresses up like a judge and stands before a mirror and sentences himself to loneliness for the rest of his life.

But, your Honor, you haven't heard my side of it...

You have no side of it; you have been found guilty of impersonating a judge and standing before a mirror admiring yourself.

I throw myself on the mercy of the court; I acted only out of loneliness...

Loneliness is no excuse for violating the law.

But, your Honor, please, I've been lonely all my life. Isn't the debt almost paid?—Not more loneliness!—I demand my sentence be shortened! I've already paid for my crime!

I make no deals with convicted criminals. If you think you can do better try another judge.

But, your Honor...

Clear the court and go to bed!

Although it is easy to get caught up in the strangeness of this seemingly comical tale, it has something very important to say about the human condition—more specifically about how we treat ourselves as human beings. It points out how we judge and sentence ourselves to the lives we are living.

Clearly, the one and only character in this prose poem has done this. He has judged himself and then sentenced himself to a life of loneliness. Although he thinks that a real judge has sentenced him, we know better. We know that the man is talking to himself while looking in a mirror after having dressed up as a judge.

Interestingly, when he looks in the mirror, he doesn't see himself. He only sees a judge. And he pleads to this judge for mercy. He says, "But, your Honor, please, I've been lonely all my life. Isn't the debt almost paid?—Not more loneliness!..." But that's exactly what the judge sentences him to: more loneliness.

Aren't we like the character in this prose poem, outwardly saying what we do not want (in this case, a life of loneliness), but inwardly sentencing ourselves to that very thing? And also like the character in this prose poem, don't we sentence ourselves based on the judgments we have about ourselves?

We may not talk to ourselves out loud while looking in the mirror. But that doesn't mean we aren't talking to ourselves silently. Nor does it mean that we are not judging ourselves and then sentencing ourselves based on our self-imposed judgments.

YOUR TURN—

What sentence have you given yourself? And what's the judgment that your sentence is based on? After you've written out your answers to these two questions, share what you've written with the people in your group.

Note: If you're like most of us, you have probably given yourself a number of different sentences. For this exercise, however, just focus on one.

CHAPTER 6

CHOOSING TO BE A VICTIM

Although you may think that no one would ever choose to be a victim, in different areas of our lives we have. We usually don't make this choice consciously. But we make it, nonetheless. And we continue to make it every time something happens that we feel powerless to do anything about.

Seeing Myself as a Victim

For years I had a story about how I became a victim. My story included having parents who were not available to me when I needed them, growing up in a working class neighborhood where kids didn't have many aspirations in life, and getting caught up in a criminal justice system that seemed to be more interested in catching people and locking them up than in helping anyone who had gone astray.

My victim story also included being bullied by the tough kids in my neighborhood, with whom I did my best to avoid, and being negatively influenced by my friends Ricky and Louis, who often did things that were against the law. The police were part of my victim-story as well. I blamed them for going after me in a high-speed chase when I was only sixteen. As for the courts, I blamed them for locking me up instead of coming up with a more humane way to rehabilitate me. But primarily, I blamed my parents for how my life turned out. I believed it was their fault for not effectively intervening to stop my wayward behavior before it had gotten out of control. I also blamed my parents for working as much as they did instead of spending quality time with my siblings and me.

My victim story had me convinced that it was the fault of all these people and institutions that my life turned out the way it did. But I don't know this with any certainty. What I do know is that I had a story that made me into a victim and other people into the problem. According to my story, it was everyone else's fault except mine that my life unfolded the way it did.

Finding Fault

It is always much easier to find fault with others and blame them for things that have gone wrong in our lives than it is to take responsibility for our lives. But finding fault with anyone—including ourselves—doesn't accomplish very much. In fact, it usually exacerbates our problems, because it forces us to focus on what's wrong with us or others instead of on what we can do to improve things.

Marshall Rosenberg, author of *Nonviolent Communication: A Language of Life,* says it's essential that we focus on people's needs rather than on their faults. Yet he recognizes that we are not trained to do this. In the paragraph below from his book, he points out how most of us have been trained to react to others who do things that we don't like or understand.

> When I encountered people or behaviors I either didn't like or didn't understand, I would react in terms of their wrongness. If my teachers assigned a task I didn't want to do, they were "mean" or "unreasonable." If someone pulled out in front of me in traffic, my reaction would be, "You idiot!" When we speak this language,

we think and communicate in terms of what's wrong with others for behaving in certain ways, or occasionally, what's wrong with ourselves for not understanding or responding as we would like. Our attention is focused on classifying, analyzing, and determining levels of wrongness rather than on what we and others need and are not getting.

There is a lot to learn from what Rosenberg is saying. When our focus is on blaming others, it is almost impossible to look at our needs and ask ourselves *What is it that is missing in our lives that is having us react the way we are reacting?* Is it love, respect, being valued or appreciated? The opportunity for us is to understand which of our needs are not being met, so we can work on getting them met.

If our focus is on blaming others—even if it's on blaming ourselves—we're not looking at our needs. All we're doing is "determining levels of wrongness."

We probably don't even know which of our needs are not being met. We also probably have no idea about what we're telling ourselves that is having us react the way we're reacting. Given this scenario, it becomes almost impossible to distinguish what it is that is having us feel the way we're feeling.

Of course, we can always blame someone for why we feel the way we do and why we're reacting the way we are. But this will not help us understand ourselves any more than we already do. Nor will it help us to have a different experience when something similar happens again.

YOUR TURN—

Think back to a time when you got upset with someone. Write down why you got upset. What was it you needed but were not able to get, and why do you think you weren't able to get it? What was it that the person you were upset with did or didn't do? And why did you react the way you reacted instead of some other way? Write down what you see about this and share what you've written with the people in your group.

A Choice: To Stay a Victim or Not

Things have happened in each one of our lives that we've had little or no control over, and they will continue to happen. We can blame others for having caused those things to have happened and remain victims, or we can take responsibility for our reaction to everything that has happened and choose our lives.

This doesn't mean we have to like everything that has happened or that the people who have said or done things that hurt us shouldn't be held accountable for the things they have said and done. All it means is that we have a choice regarding how we are going to experience life. We can be a victim or not be one.

Of course, there are things over which we have no control. And things happen that we would never choose, but we can always choose how we are going to respond to what happens.

No matter what happens, you can always ask yourself these questions: *How am I going to let this impact me? Am I going to see myself as a victim because of what has happened? Or am I going to see myself as powerful, resourceful, and responsible, no matter what has happened?*

We all have more power than we realize. We don't have to *blame* others or ourselves when things happen that we don't like. Instead, we can choose to look inside ourselves and take responsibility for our internal conversations and unmet needs. And we can do this without making ourselves or anyone else wrong.

No matter what is happening or has happened, we can hold on to what Viktor Frankl refers to as the last of the human freedoms: "to choose one's attitude in any given set of circumstances, to choose one's own way."

YOUR TURN—

Describe something that happened in your life that caused you or continues to cause you to feel like a victim. What story or stories have you made up about what happened? And who or what did or do you blame for causing those things to happen? Please write down why you blame a particular person or group of people. And share what you've written with the people in your group.

PART II

FREEING YOURSELF FROM YOUR MENTAL PRISONS: WHAT YOU CAN DO

CHAPTER 7

WHY BEING MORE SELF-AWARE MATTERS

One of the most important things any of us can do to free ourselves from our mental prisons is to become more self-aware. And the way to do this is to recognize our internal conversations as internal conversations.

Only by being aware of our internal conversations, and distinguishing them as such, will we be able to notice the affect they have on our lives and begin to understand how they keep us in the mental prisons we're in.

Freud, the Unconscious, and Me

In the early 1900s, Sigmund Freud developed a theory of personality based on people having an id, ego, and superego. He also proposed that in addition to us having a conscious mind, we also have an unconscious one, where we store information that we are not ready or able to deal with consciously.

From working with his patients, Freud discovered it was possible to access the contents of people's unconscious. And by accessing the unconscious, he realized he could help people become free of many of their mental, emotional, and psychological blocks.

Using his approach—what is known by some as talk-therapy, but is so much more—hundreds of thousands of people have been helped in psychiatrists', psychoanalysts', psychologists', and social workers' offices around the world. I have been one of these people. Meeting with a therapist for a number of years on a weekly basis helped me in so many ways. Mainly, it helped me recognize that there were things going on in my life that I was clueless about.

One of them was my anger.

I knew I would get angry when things happened that I didn't like. But I had no idea that there was an undercurrent of anger behind everything I said and did—at least, not until my therapist asked me to consider it.

In my inquiry, what became clear to me for the first time was that I was angry at myself for the things I had done as a teenager. This was new to me, because for years I had blamed my parents for the things that happened when I was a teenager. My anger had been directed at my parents for having not done a better job raising me. But in therapy it became clear to me that I was using my parents as scapegoats. They had done the best they could, given who they were and what they knew at the time. Blaming them was a way for me to avoid looking at the person I was really angry at.

This was eye-opening. It had me realize that blaming my parents for the things that happened when I was a rebellious teenager did nothing except to hurt them and me. As a result, I decided to apologize to them for having blamed them and for having cut them out of my life for the few years I did. So I apologized. Fortunately, they forgave me. And I got my parents back in my life, which was wonderful.

Another thing I did with my therapist's help was to become more conscious of my anger and notice it before it got out of control. As a result, I started to experience feeling more peaceful.

What therapy mainly did for me was to help me become much more self-aware. And this has been invaluable to me because the more self-aware I've become, the more control I have gotten over how I experience things—no matter what is going on.

From going to therapy, I realized that I didn't have to continue experiencing life like I did in the past. I could experience it very differently. And we all can. We all have the ability to change how we experience the different things that happen over the course of our lives any time we want.

There is no doubt in my mind that I got tremendous value from going to therapy while I was incarcerated and after I got out. For this reason, I cannot recommend it highly enough. It helped me uncover things about myself that I didn't even know I was covering up. And it can help anyone who's willing to do the work.

Having regular sessions with a therapist is a sure way to acquire more peace, freedom, and happiness in your life. But you do have to be willing to look at your life in a way you may have never looked at it before and take responsibility for what you find out.

If you are not ready or able to do this by working with a therapist, there are other things you can do that will also help you become more self-aware.

Some of the Other Things You Can Do

One of the other things you can do to become more self-aware is to take courses that will help with this. There are more than a few organizations and companies that have such courses. Some are even online. Two that have an online presence but also have courses that are in physical locations, which I can personally recommend, are Landmark Worldwide and the Diamond Approach.

The Diamond Approach requires membership if you want to participate in one of its local groups in person, but it also has some online courses that do not. As for Landmark Worldwide, there is no membership required. You just pay course by course. And almost all its courses are at various locations in different cities around the world.

Although each of these organizations is considerably different from one another in mission and method, and neither would market itself as being primarily about self-awareness, it would be impossible to participate in either one without becoming more self-aware. To find out more about these groups, all one has to do is look them up on the internet.

And if you are not sure whether you want to work in a group or work one-on-one with a therapist, counselor, or life-coach, below is a short list of some of the pluses and minuses of working in a group compared to working one-on-one with a professional.

The pluses of working in a group:
1) You won't be on the spot as much as you would be if you were working one-on-one with a psychotherapist, counselor, or life coach.

2) You'll have the opportunity to get feedback not just from one person, but from many.
3) It will likely cost less than working one-on-one with a trained professional.

The minuses of working in a group:
1) You will not get the same degree of focused attention you would if you were working one-on-one with a professional.
2) The group's agenda will not always be your own.
3) It will still be costly, but not quite as costly as weekly sessions with a professional.

If you are not ready or interested in working in a group or one-on-one with a therapist, counselor, or life-coach, here are few things you can do on your own to help you become more self-aware.
- Journal. You can write down your thoughts and feelings in a notebook or on your computer everyday if possible.
- Read. You can read self-help books and listen to CDs and on-line audio programs on self-awareness and personal growth.
- Meditate. You can concentrate on your breathing or use guided meditations to quiet down your mind, so

you can hear what you're saying to yourself when you don't think you're saying anything.
- Yoga. You can do yoga poses to take your focus off your mind and put it on your body. You'd be surprised by how taking your focus off you mind helps you find out things about yourself that you didn't know.

Doing any or all of these things will help you become more self-aware. And the more self-aware you become, the easier it will be to make positive changes in your life because you'll know exactly what needs changing.

YOUR TURN—

What are two insights you've had about your life in the last year? And why do you think you've had these insights when you did? What impact, if any, have they had on your life?

If you have not had any new insights about your life in the last year, why do you think that is? Please write down your answers to these questions and share what you've written with the people in your group.

A Final Word about Becoming More Self-Aware

Becoming more self-aware is one of the most important things you can do because it will help you discover things about yourself that you can change when you're ready to.

Sadly, a lot of people are not interested in doing this work because they believe that they already know everything they need to know about themselves, which is not possible because 1) we're always changing and 2) there are things in our unconscious, which we have no clue about.

This is why it's important that we work with others when we're trying to become more self-aware. Others can often see things about us that we can't see ourselves. Of course, if you're committed to finding out all you can about yourself on your own, you might be able to push beyond what you already know. But it will certainly be easier working with a professional or, at least, someone you respect and trust.

However, if you believe you already know everything you're ever going to need to know about yourself and you're not living a life you love, then you have to ask yourself what is it that is stopping you from loving the life you have. If there is nothing, great! If you think it's someone or some circumstance, then you have a choice. You can either do everything possible to change that person or circumstance and see if that works. Or you can consider that there are things you don't know about yourself that if you knew would give you more peace, freedom, and happiness in your life.

YOUR TURN—

Write down three things you already know about yourself and explain how you know them.

Also explore in your journal and with your group, one thing you can do over the next week to help you become more self-aware. After you do this one thing, discuss with your group what you learned about yourself from doing it.

CHAPTER 8

TAKING FULL RESPONSIBILITY FOR YOUR LIFE

In addition to becoming more self-aware, the other great gift you can give yourself is to become more responsible; that is, more responsible for your life than you've ever been before. In fact, it is only when you're being fully responsible for your life that you can choose it. Until that time, you may think that you are choosing your life, but your internal conversations are doing the choosing for you.

But How Does One Begin to Be Fully Responsible?

You begin by recognizing that the life you're living, as good as it is, is limited by your internal conversations.

Once you recognize this, you can distinguish the different internal conversations you are having with yourself and the impact that each of them is having on your life.

Until that time, you can't be fully responsible for your life because you don't fully know your life. Of course, you know it as well as you know it. But to be fully responsible for your life, you have to know it more than you already do. You have to know why you make the choices you do and be able to *own* all the choices you have made.

More Reasons Why Being Responsible for Your Internal Conversations Is So Important

It's so important because what you tell yourself influences your choices, and your choices shape your life. Your internal conversations are not the only things that influence your choices and shape your life. But unlike external things which you often don't have control over, you do have control over your internal conversations and your choices.

In a world where situations arise that are often beyond our control, taking responsibility for our internal conversations and the choices they guide us to make lets us have some of that control back. It reminds us that we do have a say over how we experience our lives.

Another reason being responsible for your internal conversations is so important is because when you are, you stop being a victim. That doesn't mean you don't get angry or feel upset about things that were said or done. But when you do get angry or feel upset, you can recognize it as a choice. And since it's a choice, you can decide how angry or upset you are going to be and for how long.

When you're taking responsibility for your internal conversations, you're in charge of how life shows up for you. Sure, there will be times when your emotions will take over. But if you believe you have a choice in the matter, you can control your emotions even when they initially make you feel out of control.

When you're responsible for your internal conversations, you don't have to react a particular way even if it feels familiar. You can choose how you're going to react or if you're going to react at all. Clearly, if you want more peace, freedom, and happiness in your life, the best way to achieve these things is by taking responsibility for your internal conversations and the choices they lead you to make.

What you'll notice when you're being responsible for your internal conversations is that how life occurs to you will change. You will not get as upset as you used to, if you get upset at all. There will be a feeling of peace and ease in your life that had not been there before.

But Why Should You Be Responsible for Conversations that Were Passed Down to You?

Because they're yours! If you've listened to any of them for any length of time, they've become part of your own internal guidance system.

Yes, it's true that you inherited many of your internal conversations when you were young. And at that time, you didn't have a lot of choice regarding which conversations you were and weren't going to listen to. You listened to whatever conversations your mother, father, teachers, and other people in authority told you to listen to. But if you kept listening to those conversations after you became an adult, they're yours.

It is time to acknowledge that. And the way to acknowledge it is by taking ownership of those conversations, especially the disempowering ones. And you do that by being responsible for having listened to those conversations for as long as you have and for the choices they've led you to make. It's those choices that have given you the life you have. But it's your internal conversations that have given you your choices. So if you want to change your life, start by being responsible for your internal conversations.

What Does It Mean to Be Responsible?

It means you take ownership of who you are and what you've done. You stop blaming others and you stop blaming yourself for anything that has happened in the past. You also stop pretending you're innocent or a victim.

When you're responsible for your life, you're responsible for all the things that have happened that have led you to where you are today. You recognize that the buck stops with you.

This doesn't mean you need to make yourself wrong for anything you've said or done. It also doesn't mean that you need to make others wrong. In fact, you might consider apologizing to people you have hurt.

If there is any compensation you feel that is due others because of things you've said or done and you're able to make that compensation, great! If you're not able to, perhaps you can make amends in some other way.

What is most important is that you get complete with your past as much as you can, so it does not get in the way of you achieving your dreams and accomplishing your goals. The past is the past. It can be a springboard into a new future, but it can also keep you stuck where you're at. So do what you can to be complete with it, so it's not in the way of you living a life you love.

An Affirmation

Below is an affirmation to remind you that you are more responsible than you think and that you already choose your life more than you realize. I suggest that you start by saying it to yourself a few times each day whenever you can.

> I AM RESPONSBILE FOR ALL MY INTERNAL CONVERSATIONS—THE ONES THAT EMPOWER ME AS WELL AS THE ONES THAT DON'T. I KNOW THAT I'M RESPONSIBLE FOR EVERYTHING I THINK AND BELIEVE AND FOR THE IMPACT THAT ALL MY INTERNAL CONVERSATIONS HAVE HAD AND CONTINUE TO HAVE ON MY CHOICES AND MY LIFE.

EVEN THOUGH I HAVE NOT CAUSED EVERYTHING TO HAPPEN THE WAY IT HAS, I TAKE FULL RESPONSIBILITY FOR MY EXPERIENCE OF EVERYTHING THAT HAS HAPPENED, WILL HAPPEN, AND IS HAPPENING BECAUSE I CAN.

Think of this affirmation as a tool you can use any time you want to remind you that you can always change the way you experience things, no matter what is happening or how you're feeling.

YOUR TURN—

Say the above affirmation to yourself twice a day for a week while you are looking in the mirror—preferably once in the morning and once in the evening. Then share with the people in your group what, if anything, has changed since you started saying it.

Also write down one internal conversation you have about yourself that you haven't been very responsible for and explain why you haven't been more responsible for it. Then when your group meets share with them what you're written.

Note: This is not an opportunity to make yourself wrong for not being more responsible. It's simply an opportunity to look at what has been stopping you from being as responsible as you can be.

CHAPTER 9

SEVEN KEYS TO UNLOCK THE DOORS OF YOUR MENTAL PRISONS

Here are seven keys to help you unlock the doors of your mental prisons. Use them to get out from a life that's been limiting what's possible for you. Use them, so you can experience peace, freedom, and joy in your life at a level you have never experienced peace, freedom, and joy before.

Take each key in your hand (metaphorically, of course) and use each one to unlock one more door of your mental prisons—maybe a door that you didn't even know was locked.

Key One: Know the Road You're on as the Story It Is

To have more peace, freedom, and joy in your life, it's important to know the road you're on for what it is: a well-developed story with evidence that's been carefully gathered and woven together to make all parts of it appear believable and true.

In fact, your story about your life is so believable and convincing that you probably didn't realize that *how* you think of your life is based on a story at all. It is as if the things you say happened actually happened.

Of course they did!

The issue is not about whether those things happened. It's about you recognizing that you have imposed your *interpretation* of what happened on what happened, and now relate to your interpretation as the truth.

Let's say, for example, that you didn't get a job you wanted. After thinking about it, you conclude that you didn't get the job because of your age. But you don't know this. No one told you. You only know that you didn't get the job. Nevertheless, you made up a story to explain why you didn't get it. Your story could be accurate or inaccurate, but that's not the point! The point is you made up a story that is based on an opinion that comes from your interpretation about what happened.

To use this key, you must recognize that almost everything you know about yourself, others, and the world is based on stories that are part fact and part interpretation. Only by distinguishing the part that is fact from the part that is interpretation will you be able to use this key to free yourself from what you were sure was true.

By using this key, you will know that you can create new stories based on different interpretations of the same facts all the time—each one more interesting and imaginative than the one before it.

Key Two: Stop Resisting Your Life the Way It Is

You might not love your life the way it is. You may not even *like* it the way it is, but don't be in an argument with the way it is. That is, don't tell yourself that it should be different from the way it is. It *is* the way it *is*!

Try embracing your life the way it is. You don't have to like it being this way, but you don't have to be in a battle with it being the way it is either. If you resist your life or any part of it being the way it is, you're in a battle with your life. And this can be exhausting, not to mention self-defeating.

It is time to put down your weapons and get off the battlefield. Choose your life the way it is for no other reason than you can and already have.

Key Three: Choose to Get to the Heart of the Matter

Speak from your heart, whether speaking from your heart looks good or not. There is a lot you can learn about yourself when you are willing to be vulnerable and speak from your heart. This may mean getting in touch with parts of yourself that you'd rather not—those parts of yourself that show up as hurt, angry, childish, or foolish.

So what! How else are you going to be aware of what's going on with you if you're not in touch with all the different parts of yourself?

By using this key, you get to embrace those parts of you that operate on a different plane than the logical brain does.

Key Four: Choose to Forgive Yourself and Others

Many people remain upset in the present for things that have happened in the past. However, life is moving forward. Shouldn't you move forward with it? The way to do this is by forgiving everyone you have ever blamed for anything that's happened.

But before you start forgiving others, begin by forgiving yourself. Forgive yourself for all the things you have ever said or done that hurt other living beings. (And don't think you haven't. We all have.) This includes forgiving yourself for having hurt yourself.

Being upset, angry, and unforgiving for things that have happened is baggage you can choose to carry with you or put down. It's your baggage with a leash on it, and it will follow you wherever you go until you put it down.

Choose forgiveness. Choose to give everyone a fresh start, including yourself. People did whatever they did, just as you've done the things you've done. There is nothing that you or others have said or done that is so awful it cannot be forgiven. *Nothing!* So choose forgiveness. Once you do, you'll be able to move on with your life without having to carry your baggage with you wherever you go.

Key Five: Choose to Step Outside of Your Comfort Zone and Take Risks

Imagine what's possible when you step outside of your comfort zone and start saying and doing things you have never said or done before.

Invent, create, and discover new roads that will lead you to new destinations. Start exploring the uncharted paths that only *you* can discover. Take risks that will move you in the direction of your dreams. Choose to soar, even if you've never soared before. Use this key to go beyond the familiar, to experience life as fully as you can.

Key Six: Choose Your Life and Celebrate It

Many people tolerate their lives, but only a small number of us celebrate them. What a great opportunity you have to appreciate and celebrate your life, no matter what has happened in the past or is happening now. You can choose to celebrate all of it, including those parts you'd rather not.

In his book of poems, *Leaves of Grass*, Walt Whitman, the father of American poetry, starts his famous poem "Song of Myself" with the line, "I celebrate myself, and sing myself." Whitman knew the importance of celebrating his life and all of life.

He also knew the importance of living a life of choice. In his poem "Song of the Open Road," he writes,

> Afoot and light-hearted I take to the open road,
> Healthy, free, the world before me,
> The long brown path before me leading wherever I choose.

Why don't you heed Whitman's words and go wherever you choose? The fact is you're already on the path you've chosen. It has brought you to where you are today and is leading you to wherever you are ready to go next. Even if you're not sure exactly where that is, you are on the way. The only thing you have to do is take the next step and celebrate your life with every step you take.

Key Seven: Let Others Choose for Themselves

It's important to let adults who are mature and capable enough to think for themselves make their own choices, no matter how much you may want to intervene and tell them what choices you think they should make.

Of course, when it comes to children, you do have to make many choices for them. You have to guide them until they are able to take responsibility for their own lives and make intelligent choices for themselves. And when they are able, you will want to get out of the way, so they *can* make their own choices. The power of choice is an awesome power, and it's our privilege to pass it on.

Nevertheless, there will be times—probably many times—when you think you know what the best choice for another is. You might even decide to stop communicating with a person you care about just because you disagree with that person's choices. It could happen that you get into a full-blown argument with a spouse, a friend, or a relative because you dislike some of the choices one of these people has made. But where does this get you? Where does it get any of us when we insist that people choose the things we want them to choose instead of letting each person make his or her own choices?

There's not much room for growth and development when any of us get into a serious argument and stop communicating with someone we know just because we disagree with that person's choices. It's important, therefore, that we do everything we can to keep communication open, find common ground, and stay related.

Instead of engaging in the conversations *I know better* or *that person made a terrible choice*, we can acknowledge that each of us is different. And each of us is going to make different choices. The opportunity for all of us is to honor and respect other people's choices as we encourage others to honor and respect ours.

Yes, we want to be able to tell people why we think making certain choices is better than making others. But if we try to *force* anyone to make the choices we want them to make, they will not feel understood, appreciated, or respected. And they will probably not understand, appreciate, or respect us and the choices we make either.

CHAPTER 10

FIVE PRACTICES TO CREATE A LIFE YOU LOVE

In addition to using the Seven Keys to unlock the doors of your mental prisons, here are Five Practices to help you create a life you love. Please do the practices daily and focus on a different one each week.

Practice #1: Get Clear about Your Vision

Make time each day to envision a future that fulfills and delights you. You don't have to know exactly what this future looks like. But take time imagining different ways it may look and feel until you have a sense of it that pleases you.

YOUR TURN— *the Practice for week 1*

Take five to ten minutes each day for a week to imagine what living a life you love looks and feels like. Focus on what it feels like even more than what it looks like. Describe your ideal life in writing, and then share what you've written with the people in your group.

If you are not able to envision what living a life you love looks and feels like, consider that your internal conversations are getting in your way. Use one or more members of your group to explore how your internal conversations are stopping you from envisioning your ideal life.

Practice #2: Believe You Can Live a Life You Love

Take time each day to believe that you *can* live a life you love. If you don't believe you can, it is doubtful you will do the things you need to do to have that life show up.

Imagine if the Wright brothers didn't believe man could fly or if Thomas Edison didn't believe he could create an incandescent light bulb. We might still be earthbound and living in the dark.

You must believe you can accomplish what you want to accomplish in order to set about accomplishing it. Believing that something is possible is necessary to bring that something into existence.

YOUR TURN— *the Practice for week 2*

Take five to ten minutes each day for the second week believing you can live a life you love. One way to do this is by saying to yourself in the mirror at least twice a day, "I believe I can live a life I love." After you say it, take a few minutes to consider what you said. And at the end of each day, record what—if anything—showed up that might be related to your practice in the mirror. If possible find a person from your group to share with at the end of each day.

Practice #3: Be Willing to Live a Life You Love

In addition to believing you can live a life you love, you have to be willing to do what it takes to live that life. If you're not willing, the game is over before it's begun.

So ask yourself, are you willing to work on yourself and be open to discovering things about yourself that you didn't already know? Are you willing to change beliefs you've held for years if you recognize that some of them are not helping you get any closer to living a life you love? If you are, great! And if you're not, ask yourself, why not? What's stopping you? Why aren't you willing to do whatever you can to start living a life you love today?

YOUR TURN— *the Practice for week 3*

Every day for the third week take five to ten minutes to write down what you are and are not willing to do to live a life you love. Find one person from your group to share this with each day. And when your group meets share what you've written with them as well.

Practice #4: Be in Action to Live a Life You Love

The fourth practice is to be in action, which means you need to do things—things that will bring you closer to achieving your goals and fulfilling your dreams. There may be hundreds of different things you can do, depending on what your goals and dreams are. But start by doing *one* thing.

For your life to change, you have to be in action to change it. If you do nothing, your life will stay the same. If you do just a little, only a little is going to change. Of course, little changes are fine to begin with. Before you know it, they will have added up to some big changes. But don't be afraid to make big changes either. If at all possible, make both big and little changes whenever you can.

Being in action is a powerful practice because it sets things in motion that were not in motion before. It will take you outside your comfort zone. And when you go outside your comfort zone, life as you've known it changes.

YOUR TURN— *the Practice for week 4*

Take one action every day for the fourth week. They can be big or small actions. After you take each one, write down what you did, what it was like doing what you did, and how having done what you did has or hasn't brought you closer to living a life you love.

Also find one person in your group with whom you can share your results at the end of each day. Of course, also share what you've written with the people in your group when you meet.

Practice #5: Be Intentional to Live a Life You Love

The last practice, being intentional, has to do with putting your focus and energy on thinking about and visualizing what you want to accomplish and create. It's bringing your intentions into conscious awareness.

Lynne McTaggart, author of *The Intention Experiment*, believes that if you are clear about your intentions and able to focus on them, you can direct your thoughts and energies towards having your intentions realized.

In her book, McTaggart refers to numerous occasions in which injured and sick people healed themselves and athletes won sporting events through the power of intention. To have this happen, she writes that the intention must be formulated as a very specific aim or goal. And you must think about it as if it has already been accomplished.

YOUR TURN— *the Practice for week 5*

Take five to ten minutes every day for the fifth week to intend something to happen that will move you closer to living a life you love. Then at the end of each day, write down what, if anything, happened and share that with one person from your group. And when your group meets, share what you've written with all of them.

If you are having problems doing any of these practices, use the people in your group to help you explore which of your internal conversations are getting in your way.

PART III

GOING BEYOND THE FAMILIAR: WHAT'S POSSIBLE

CHAPTER 11

CREATING FROM THE UNKNOWN

It's important to be able to create from the unknown because things are possible in the unknown that are not possible in the known. But to do this you have to be present in the moment and open to whatever shows up. If you are living in the past, continually referencing what you already know, what is going to show up will simply be more of what you already know.

What's Wrong with Coming from What We Already Know?

On many levels, nothing! In fact, we need to be able to come from what we already know for many reasons. One is so we all have a shared experience of reality. If we all come from what we already know when we say something, others will know what we mean. We also need to come from what we know, so we can build on it. Imagine if every time we went to work, we'd have to learn our jobs over again even though we've been doing the same job for years. We also need to come from what we already know to have a sense of who we are. The way we know ourselves is by looking at our history, at what we already know about ourselves.

There is no question that we need to be able to come from what we already know and be able to use that knowledge in our lives. In fact, there is almost no way not to. However, it's important to recognize that coming from what we already know can and, often, does limit us. It has us focus on the past more than the present. And when we're focused on the past—on what we already know—it's impossible to be fully present.

And when we're not fully present, we miss things that are happening right before our eyes. We miss the newness that is inherent in every moment.

T.S. Eliot, one of the great modernist poets, describes the problem this way in this passage from his long poem *Four Quartets:*

> There is, it seems to us
> At best, only a limited value
> In the knowledge derived from experience.
> The knowledge imposes a pattern, and falsifies,
> For the pattern is new in every moment
> And every moment is a new and shocking
> Valuation of all we have been.

From this passage, it is clear that Eliot believes that the knowledge derived from experience is limiting because it "imposes a pattern, and falsifies." It falsifies because "the pattern is new in every moment/And every moment is a new and shocking/Valuation of all we have been."

Yet most of us don't realize this or recognize it. We think one moment is like the next. It certainly appears that way to us. But each moment is unique and has never been experienced before even if it seems exactly like the moment before it.

Until we recognize this, we will never be fully present in the moment. We will always be lingering in the past, using our knowledge from past experiences to relate to what is happening today when what is happening today has never happened before, no matter how similar it appears to be. The bottom line is that if we remain focused on the knowledge derived from past experiences and inherited conversations, we are going to miss a lot.

What's Possible When We Are Totally Present?

Everything! Because when we are completely present, we are in the unknown. And when we are in the unknown, we are free—free to create and free to explore. We are not locked into the past or any knowledge derived from the past.

We could say that Malcolm X, the well-known African-American leader who was gunned down in his prime, came from the unknown when he reinvented himself as a self-educated authority on race relations. How else could he have gone from being a thief to becoming a leader for so many people?

Here was a man who had been arrested and locked up for burglary. He was not someone you'd expect to become an authority on race relations with an autobiography that would be read by millions. But while he was incarcerated he made some choices that would change his life forever. One was to become a Muslim. Another was to learn every word in the English dictionary.

To do these things, he had to have been able to free himself from his past, so he could be totally in the present. If he had been locked into past beliefs about himself and the world, it is doubtful he would have been able to step outside of them to become a Muslim and begin learning every word in the English dictionary. Doing both of these things required him to be in the present.

As Malcolm X wrote down each new word and studied the sentences that demonstrated how each word should be used, I imagine his internal conversations had to have been screaming at him to stop. I can almost hear them saying to him in a condescending tone: *Who do you think you are that you need to know all these words? Do you think that knowing any more words will actually make a difference in your life? You'll still be a criminal. You'll still be behind bars.*

If his internal conversations were saying these things to him inside his head, he certainly didn't let them stop him because he continued learning word after word until he got through the entire dictionary. And he didn't let his internal conversations stop him from becoming a Muslim and a leader for the African American people either.

Malcolm X may have been informed by his past, but he certainly wasn't imprisoned by it. Had he been, he would not have been able to recreate himself in the present. He would not have been able to step outside his comfort zone and become someone he didn't know he could be, which is exactly what he did. He created a brand new life for himself—a life that was not chained down by beliefs he had about himself based on the past.

And this is something we all can and must do if we are committed to reinventing ourselves and choosing to live lives we love. We must step outside of our comfort zone and discover what's possible.

Of course, like Malcolm X, you will want to be informed by your past. But also like him, you won't want to be limited by it. You certainly won't want be stuck in it or bogged down by it. You will want to be able to mine it for its gold without letting the gold weigh you down and stop you from discovering what's next once you step outside of your mental prison walls.

CHAPTER 12

FINDING THE SUPPORT YOU NEED

Do not take this journey you're on to recreate your life all by yourself. It's important to share your experiences with others. The more you share what's happening and what you're up to with others, the easier it will be to get to where you're going.

Granted, not everyone will understand or appreciate what you're doing or why you're doing it. That's why it's important to take the time to explain to as many people as you can how you got on the path you're on and where you're heading. The more people who know these things about you, the more people you'll have to draw on for support and the clearer you'll be about your own journey.

The Kind of People You're Looking For

Although you'll want as many people as possible to know about the journey you're on, the people you'll want to call on for support will be of a special kind. For one thing, they will be people who recognize the importance of being self-aware and responsible for their internal conversations and choices. For another, they'll be committed to finding out what stops them in life, so they can move beyond whatever that is.

These people will not be interested in playing the "blame game," nor will they be interested in any "poor me" stories. They will be people committed to living fulfilling and inspiring lives moment by moment, and they'll do everything they possibly can to do that. Actually, they'll do everything they possibly can, so all people can do that.

The people you'll want to support you on the journey you're on will be people who embrace change and do not settle for business as usual. They will be people who take risks, trust themselves, and fail. Yes, the people you'll want to support you on your journey will have failed at any number of things. They will have also been afraid, resigned, and confused. What will differentiate them from others, however, is that they didn't stop when they were afraid, resigned, or confused. They kept going.

They continued to move in the direction of their dreams even when their internal conversations did everything to stop them.

These people are leaders in their own right. After talking to them for a short while, you will know that they are not following the herd but forging their own paths—ever aware that to have the kind of lives they want to live and the kind of world they want to live in, they have to be at work creating it and enrolling others in what they're creating.

These are the kind of people you'll want around you to support you as you consciously create your life from choice. They will listen carefully to what you have to say and share with you what they know. But they will not always tell you what you *want* to hear. Count on them, however, to tell you what you *need* to hear.

Where to Find the People to Support You

You will find the people to support you on your journey in trusted friends, teachers, and family members, as well as in ministers, rabbis, priests, Zen masters, clerics, and gurus. You'll find them in therapy groups, women's groups, men's groups, and 12 Step programs.

You'll find them in companies like Landmark Worldwide and in spiritual groups like the Diamond

Approach. You'll find them in people who participate in Neuro-Linguistic Programming, Silva Mind Control, Emotional Freedom Techniques, and Nonviolent Communication. You'll also find them in organizations that are committed to making the world a kinder and more environmentally friendly place like the Environmental Defense Fund, the ASPCA, The World Wildlife Fund, The Natural Resources Defense Council, PETA, Defenders of Wildlife, The Humane Society, Greenpeace, Physicians Committee for Responsible Medicine, Oxfam, UNICEF, and other similar groups.

In addition, you'll find them in coaches, counselors, and therapists. And in organizations that are involved in mentoring children, feeding the hungry, housing the homeless, and providing free medical assistance to people in need. Organizations like Big Brothers, Big Sisters, The Children's Aid Society, Make-A-Wish Foundation, SmileTrain, Doctors Without Borders, and Habitat for Humanity are only a few of hundreds of organizations where you will find the kind of people you'll want to support you on this journey you're on.

Actually, you'll find the kind of people you'll want to support you almost everywhere you look. It will be up to you, however, to choose the particular people you want on your team.

CHAPTER 13

YOU ARE THE ONE

You really are. You make a bigger difference on this planet than you realize. Every person you interact with is impacted by you. Animals too! You may not think much about the difference you make, but you ought to because you are impacting every living being on this planet by everything you think, say, and do.

Acknowledge Yourself

If you have not been acknowledged for the difference you make, please acknowledge yourself now. Perhaps you've donated money to a worthy cause or given your time volunteering at a food bank, a hospital, or some other place that depends on volunteers. Maybe you've helped animals by feeding them or taking them in. Maybe you smiled at someone who had been having a difficult day. And because you did, this person relaxed enough to smile back.

Whether it's one person or ten thousand or one animal or ten thousand, if you have contributed to one living being, you've made a huge difference on this planet—a lot bigger difference than you probably know, for there is nothing more important than helping others survive and thrive. So acknowledge yourself for this and for caring enough to want to improve your own life as well. It's not everyone who values themselves enough to work on improving the quality of their life. By doing this, you become a model for others. You become a beacon of light, pointing the way to what's possible for us all.

You are The One whether you recognize this or not! There is no one else quite like you—no one with the same talents, abilities, and history that you have. No one with the same knowledge, experience, and perspective.

You are The One—The One to show us what's possible when we believe in ourselves and help others believe in themselves too. If you have a dream for the future, do not give up on it no matter what obstacles may get in your way. Of course, be kind and compassionate as you go for your dream. And remember, most of the obstacles in your way are internal, even though it often doesn't appear that way.

YOUR TURN—

Write down two ways you have positively impacted the lives of others. Then share what you've written with the people in your group.

(Please include animals as part of the lives of others.)

Each of Us Is Neo

If you've seen the science fiction movie *The Matrix* or its two sequels, you'll remember the hero, Neo. He starts out as an ordinary guy living in a future time when machines run the world. And he ends up with extraordinary powers and a commitment to save the human race.

We may not know the exact moment in *The Matrix* when Neo chooses to embrace what his new friends have been telling him, that he is The One—The One to free the human race from the tyranny of the machines—but he does embrace it. And when he does, reality as he's known it changes.

However, Neo starts out having no idea what's possible for him or what he's capable of. Even after he has swallowed the red pill and learns that the world is being run by machines, he still doesn't know what he can do with this information.

He doesn't know what he can do and is capable of doing until he finds out that his friend Morpheus is in serious danger. It is then that he decides to do everything he can to save his friend's life.

Even though his new friends have been telling him since they met him that he is The One, it takes his friend's life being threatened for Neo to step out of his comfort zone and use his newly discovered knowledge and power to save Morpheus's life. It is then that Neo becomes this person he has not known himself to be before.

When Neo steps into the unknown to save Morpheus's life, his life transforms. He is able to dodge bullets coming straight at him and hold up a falling helicopter with a rope. Ultimately, he succeeds at rescuing Morpheus even though the odds are stacked against him.

Of course, *The Matrix* is a science fiction movie. And we know that only characters in a movie can have the kind of powers that Neo has. But in many ways we are not that different from Neo. For we too have powers we don't know we have. And like Neo, we too can transform our lives in a moment when we feel compelled to.

It is true that we are not able to stop bullets coming straight at us by holding up our hands or hold up a falling helicopter with a rope. But like Neo we too can save lives and probably already have.

You are The One. Whether or not you believe this, there is no one else quite like you. No one who has the same understanding, drive, and commitment you have. There is no one who can do exactly what you can the way you can.

Make no mistake about it the world needs you. It needs your voice, your energy, and your insights. It needs you to make the kind of difference only you can make.

Yes, it will be challenging for you to step outside your comfort zone. But if you don't, you will stay stuck where you are. Nothing is wrong with that, but there is so much more available to you in the unknown.

Why not go for it? Why not choose to live the kind of life you are capable of living and discover who you can be in the process?

You really are The One. And all you have to do right now is choose to believe it. If you do, things will become possible that had not been possible before. You will discover that like Neo, you also have powers, talents, and abilities you never realized you had and that the world has more to offer you than you ever imagined.

You've Done It

You've almost reached the last page of this book. Thank you for getting here, for reading all you've read, thinking all you've thought, writing all you've written, and sharing all you've shared. Thank you, especially, for choosing to look at your life through different lenses than you've used to look at it before, and for being willing to recognize the huge impact that your internal conversations, stories, beliefs, and judgments have on the choices you make, and the even bigger impact that your choices have on your life and on the lives of those around you.

Here are the last three *Your Turn* questions. Please answer them as thoughtfully, thoroughly, and generously as you can.

YOUR TURN—

What will you do to be more aware, conscious, and responsible for your life from this day forward?

What does the life you want to create look and feel like now?

And how will the world be different when it is the way you want it to be?

As always, write out your answers to the questions and share what you've written with the people in your group. You may also want to share what you've written with people outside your group, so you can begin bringing new people onto your team.

CHAPTER 14

SOME FINAL ADVICE

Surround yourself with people who honor, respect, and love you. Discover yourself through their eyes. Let them be your cheering section, cheering you on to greater and greater heights.

If you think you already know everything you need to know about yourself, others, and the world, no one will be able to contribute to you. So be open to the possibility that there are things you do not know and be willing to listen and learn.

Growth and development takes being in communication with others, which means you need to be in relationship with others. It also requires contributing to others and letting others contribute to you, so take the time you need to listen to what others have to say. Even if you are convinced that some people have nothing of importance to tell you, listen to them as if they do.

When you listen for great things from others, you will find them. And whether or not you believe it, others are listening for great things from you. Don't underestimate anyone. Most importantly, don't underestimate yourself!

Trust yourself, even though you will make mistakes. When you recognize you've made some, acknowledge that you have, forgive yourself, and try not to make those same or similar mistakes again. If you attempt to hide the fact that you've made mistakes, they'll show up when you least expect it.

On the other hand, if you dwell too much on your mistakes, you'll stay stuck in the past, beating yourself up for things that are over and done with. Most of us have been punished enough for things that have happened in our past. It's not necessary to punish ourselves any more. The opportunity for all of us is to forgive ourselves along with any people who have hurt us, so we can move on with our lives. Besides, nothing has happened in the past that is so terrible it cannot be forgiven. Nothing!

You now have the tools, keys, and practices you need to help you free yourself from your mental prisons. If you're not sure you remember what they all are or how to use them, consider going through the book again. Or go to my website at www.YouCanChooseYourLife.com for additional information and support.

Whatever you choose to do next, whether it's adopting a pet from a shelter to save an animal's life or being more joyful at work and at home, so the people around you smile and laugh more, keep doing what you're doing. Keep making a positive difference for as many lives as you can. From the checkout person at the supermarket to your friends, family, and pets, you make a greater difference than you realize.

You are The One. You really are. But you may need reminders about this from time to time, so find people who will remind you and welcome them into your world.

You are an incredible human being. Come out, so we know what you're up to in life. Come out, so we can celebrate who you are for us all.

And do not doubt for a second that you are whole and complete just the way you are. Any doubt about this comes from a story you inherited or made up that doesn't serve you. It is time to take responsibility for that story, so it no longer runs your life. It is time to take responsibility for all the things you tell yourself and believe, so they are not in the way of you choosing to live the life you love.

ACKNOWLEDGMENTS

There are many people I'd like to thank and acknowledge for their contributions to this book. I will start with the people who edited the book with a heavy hand. They include Mary Beans, Libbie Simonton, Ivory Krooler, Marcela Brusa, Ted Moore, MarySue Foster, and Ella Wilson. The book was also professionally edited by Simon Whaley on behalf of Capucia Publishing, Nancy Black of Mercury Press, and Nancy Marriott of New Paradigm Writing and Editing Services. Nancy Marriott also came up with the organization for the book and the title for which I'm especially grateful.

Although there are many, I want to thank all the people who have read the book in whole or in part in its early drafts and offered their comments and support. They include Dr. Don Loeffler, Jonnie Wimmer, Joel Gallob, Mary Griffin, Donna Runion, Kent McLaughlin, Stephen Dunn, Reverend Jeanie Brosius, Virginia Truman,

Betty Rivero, Lora Reaves, Mo and Michael Osterman, Stan Carpenter, Beth Schreiber, Lynn Atkinson, Dr. Cris Roberson, Rod Schwartz, Stephen Levine, Stephen Lane Taylor, Magi Speelpenning, Andi Bednar, Cheryl Moore, Dip Basu, Karen Johnson, Marilyn Sutherland, Chris Trelawny-Ross, Karin Anderson, Dorothy Scher, Phyliss Minn, Reverends Chuck and Sunnie Murphy, Lori Mackenzie, Pedro Lopez, Mary Kroncke, Dylan Stafford, Jamie Wheeler, Cooper Matlock Tama Kieves, and Geoff Affleck.

In addition, my thanks go out to my high school English teacher, Mr. Greenhouse, who opened the way for me to get my first poem published in the DeWitt Clinton High School Yearbook. This seemingly small act of kindness, which wasn't small at all, let me know that someone thought my writing was worth publishing. It was tremendously validating.

My thanks also go out to Howard Seeman who counseled me while I briefly attended DeWitt Clinton High School. He was the first teacher/counselor who took time outside of the classroom to find out what was going on with me. He introduced me to another faculty member, Miss Meehan, who also met with me outside of the classroom to offer her guidance and support. One evening she took me to Boys Town in Dobbs Ferry, New York, to speak to a Christian Father who was known for being successful in helping troubled youths. She, the Father, and all the people standing for me during my turbulent, teenage years were making a profound difference in my life, even though they may not have known it at the time. Without their help and support, I doubt I would have been able to change the path I was on.

In memory of Paul Himmel, a genuinely caring human being, who, while I was incarcerated, helped me realize that there was a whole other side of me that I wasn't in touch with—an intelligent, thoughtful, and sensitive side. He was an excellent social worker and a great listener. He met with me once a week in Rikers Island for close to a year, and I was able to share with him almost everything that was on my mind—something I didn't do with anyone else at the time. He made my stay behind bars more than bearable by providing me with the trust and support many inmates never receive.

There was also my caring parole officer, Leo Levy. I was very fortunate to have had a parole officer who appreciated me, believed in me, and spurred me on as I passed class after class in college with A and B grades. Another person I must acknowledge is Bert Weinblatt, psychologist *extraordinaire*. He helped me recognize areas in my life where I was suffering and didn't know it. With his guidance and support, I was able to lessen the suffering, and in many instances, put an end to it completely.

My thanks also go out to numerous people who were part of the Sullivanian Community in New York City. I learned a great deal from their experiment in community living and their commitment to living life to the fullest.

There are also the many professors I had at Lehman College, City College, John Jay College, the Graduate Center, the University of Texas at Dallas, and Richland College who made huge contributions to my life by sharing their knowledge and humanity with me. In addition, I thank the many teachers, advisors, supervisors, and administrators I've worked with over the years who have been my colleagues and friends. Their support and kindness cannot be matched. I must also mention the Dallas Meditation Center for all the support and wisdom I've gleaned from being part of that community.

Three more people—counselors—who positively impacted my life with their extraordinary ability to listen and contribute are Judy Minkin, Mitch Jacobs, and Deborah Leibensberger, all whom I met at Jewish Family Services in Dallas, Texas. I also thank Reverends Chuck and Sunnie Murphy and Karen Johnson along with the many other congregants at the Unity Church of Richardson for their generosity, kindness, friendship, and support. In addition, I thank Ministers Aaron White, Daniel Kanter, and Beth Dana from the Unitarian Universalist Church in Dallas for their sermons on social justice, peace, and equality; and I thank Rabbi Epstein from the Dallas Area Torah Association for inviting me to synagogue on high holy days.

Dylan Stafford, Lisa Moraski, Stephen Levine, Stephen Dunn, my sisters Cheryl Moore, Gail Rocklin, and Ivory Krooler, and my aunt and uncle Trudy and Neil Boodman deserve a big thank you as well for supporting me in getting this book finished. And I'd be remiss if I didn't mention Kathi Wittkamper, Andrea Long, Alexandra Jones, Amy McHargue, Michelle Garner, and Ryan Delp from iUniverse and Carrie Jareed and Christine Kloser from Transformation Books, now Capucia Publishing—all who guided me in getting the book ready for publication. Their help was much needed and is much appreciated.

Dusty from Office Max deserves my thanks as well for making copy after copy of early drafts of the manuscript as he shared his story with me about a brother of his who was incarcerated and who he thought would get a lot of value from reading a book like this.

To be complete, I also want to thank the leaders, staff, and participants at Landmark Worldwide, formerly Landmark Education. From them, I've learned more than I could ever convey in any book. I thank them for having me realize that transforming our lives is a lifelong process that is available to all of us all the time.

Every one of us can—and I think *should*—be continually engaged in choosing to live happier, more fulfilling, and more meaningful lives, no matter how much we've convinced ourselves that things are fine the way they are. They can always be finer.

In addition, I'd like to thank the teachers in the Diamond Approach. They have shown me that there is much more to life than meets the eye.

Of course, I couldn't have finished this book without the support of my family and friends. Nor could I have done it without my pets. They have provided me with a sense of peace, love, and comfort that kept me going as I edited and re-edited page after page. I'd also like to acknowledge the people in my men's group. It is incredible to have a small cadre of like-minded travelers to share one's journey with.

Lastly, I thank the people in the Wisdom area of Landmark Worldwide. It was from completing the Wisdom curriculum that I got the opportunity to create a promise from which I now live my life today. That promise is that *By 2042, we are all living in a world where all life is honored, respected, safe, and free.*

Imagine if that were the world we were living in today. It could be. All we need to do is roll up our sleeves and get to work. Are you ready?

BIBLIOGRAPHY: BOOKS AND FILMS

Edson, Russell. "The Judgment" in *The Intuitive Journey and Other Works*. New York: Harper & Row, 1976.

Eliot, T.S., "Little Gidding" in *Four Quartets*. New York: Harcourt, Brace & World, Inc., 1971.

Frankl, Victor E. *Man's Search for Meaning: An Introduction to Logotherapy*. New York: Simon & Schuster, 1984.

McTaggart, Lynne. *The Intention Experiment: Using Your Thoughts to Change Your Life and the World*. New York: Free Press, 2007.

Rosenberg, Marshall B. *Nonviolent Communication: A Language of Life*. California: Puddle Dancer Press, 2005.

The Matrix. Dir. Andy Wachoski and Larry Wachowski. Warner Bros. & Village Roadshow Pictures, 1999. DVD.

Whitman, Walt. "Song of Myself," and "Song of the Open Road," in *Leaves of Grass*. New York: W.W. Norton & Company, Inc., 1965.

X, Malcolm, and Alex Haley, *The Autobiography of Malcolm X*. New York: Ballantine Books, 1964.

Will You Post a Review on Amazon?

If you like what you've read in
You Can Choose Your Life,
I invite you to post a review of the
book on Amazon. This way others
who see your review might decide to buy
the book and read it too.

Thank you for your support.

Here is the link to the Amazon review page:
https://www.amazon.com/product-reviews/B07PPWKC4K

Made in the USA
Monee, IL
20 August 2021